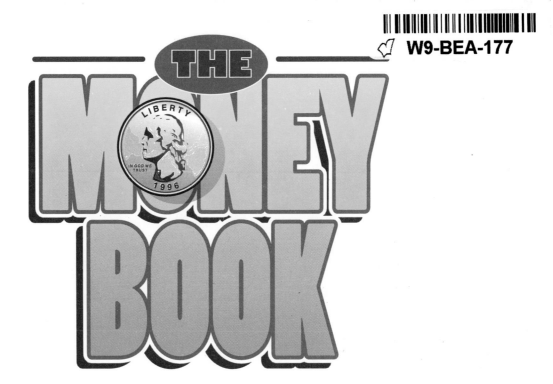

THE MONEY BOOK

Written by Elise Richards
Illustrated by Shelley Dieterichs
Cover by A. Kerr

Troll

Copyright © 1997 by Troll Communications L.L.C.

Printed in the United States of America. ISBN 0-8167-4296-0

10 9 8 7 6 5 4 3 2 1

Coins made in China

"Dad, can I buy that fish?" Jennie asked her father, pointing to a beautiful fish swimming in a tank at the pet store. It would make a perfect friend for the fish she already had at home.

"Yes, but only if you use your own money," replied her dad.

Jennie put her hand into her pocket and pulled out all her money. She had lots of coins.

Jennie walked up to the counter and laid out all the money. "I'd like to buy that fish, please," she said to the storekeeper.

"The fish costs four dollars," the storekeeper replied. "You only have forty-six cents."

"How much more do I need?" asked Jennie.

"Three dollars and fifty-four cents," said the shopkeeper.

Jennie turned to her father. "How can I get three dollars and fifty-four cents?" she asked.

"You usually save part of your allowance. When we get home, why don't you open your piggy bank to see how much money you've saved?" he suggested.

In her room, Jennie dumped all the money out of her piggy bank, then added the forty-six cents from her pocket to the pile.

She frowned. There was more money now, but Jennie didn't know whether or not it was enough to buy the fish.

Just then, Jennie's big sister, Robin, came into the room. "What are you doing, Jennie?" Robin asked.

"I need four dollars, but I can't tell how much money I have," said Jennie, looking at the money lying in front of her.

"Counting money is easy!" said Robin. "Here, let me show you how to do it."

"This is a penny," began Robin, placing a coin on the desk. "It's worth one cent. And the word *cent* is written like a lowercase 'c' with a little line on the top and another on the bottom." She drew a symbol next to the coin.

"What if you have more than one penny?" asked Jennie.

"Then you count them to see how much they're worth," explained Robin. "See, if you have three pennies, then you count one . . . two . . . three cents."

"I understand," said Jennie. "The more pennies you have, the more cents they are worth when you put them all together."

"That's right!" said Robin. Then she put down another coin. "This is the next coin. It's called a nickel, and it's worth five cents."

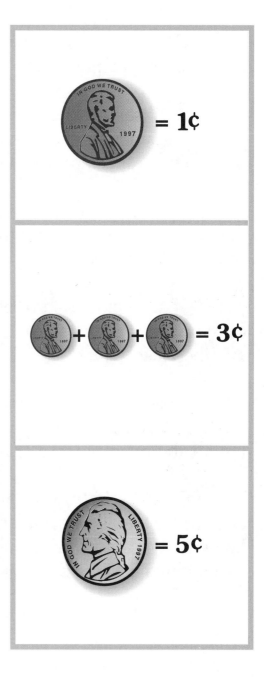

"That's the same as five pennies, right?" asked Jennie.

"Yes," said Robin. She placed five pennies next to the nickel. "See? These two groups are the same."

"I get it!" exclaimed Jennie. "They're the same because they are both worth five cents."

"That's right!" said Robin. "Now, can you count up those five pennies and the nickel all together?"

Jennie counted. "Five for the nickel . . . and six, seven, eight, nine, ten for the pennies. That's ten cents."

"Right!" said Robin. "And there's also a coin that is worth ten cents all by itself. It's called a dime," she said, laying down another coin.

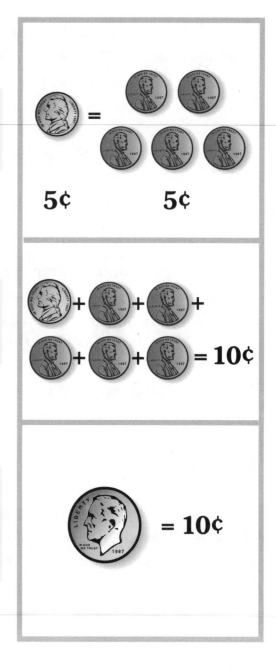

"If the dime is worth ten cents, then that must mean it's worth the same amount as this," said Jennie, pointing to the five pennies and the nickel.

"It is," said Robin. "It's also worth the same amount as two nickels, or ten pennies. You can combine coins in lots of ways to make different amounts."

"So how do I count up dimes?" asked Jennie.

"You count them by tens," replied Robin. "If you have three dimes . . ."

". . . then you count ten, twenty, thirty—thirty cents!" finished Jennie.

"You've got it!" said Robin.

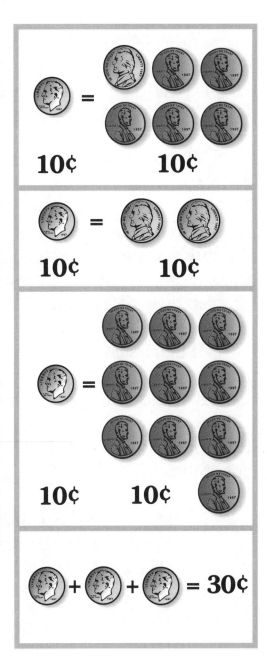

"Now here is the next coin—a quarter. It's the biggest coin you have, and it's worth the most, too. A quarter is worth twenty-five cents."

"That's a lot of pennies!" said Jennie.

Robin laughed. "Yes, it is! But it's easier to use nickels and dimes to show a quarter. There are lots of ways to make twenty-five cents."

"I understand!" said Jennie happily. But then she frowned as she looked at the coins laid out before her. "I know there are lots of cents here. But I need four dollars. How do I count those?"

"That's simple!" Robin smiled. "A dollar is one hundred cents, and it's drawn like an 'S' with a line through it." Robin drew the symbol on the paper.

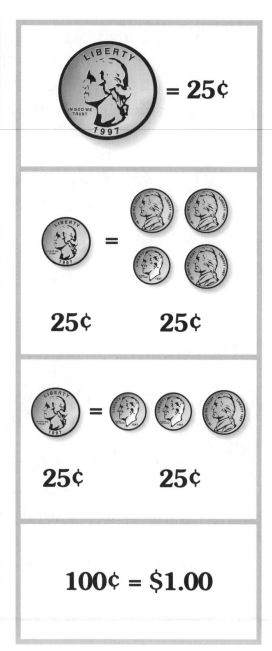

= 25¢

25¢   25¢

25¢   25¢

100¢ = $1.00

"The easiest way to make a dollar is by counting up quarters. Four quarters make one dollar. But you can also make a dollar out of any combination of coins that adds up to one hundred cents."

"Like ten dimes?" asked Jennie.

"Yes!" said Robin. "You could also just use a dollar bill, or one dollar." She took a dollar out of her pocket. "A dollar bill is the same as one hundred cents."

"So I could put my money in stacks worth one dollar each, and when I had four stacks, I would have four dollars—enough to buy my fish!" Jennie said excitedly.

"That's right, Jennie!" said Robin. "Why don't you try it now?"

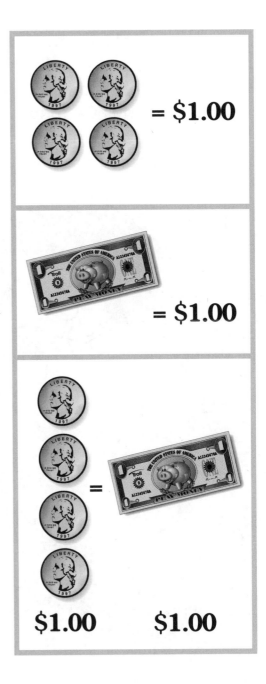

Jennie looked at the money spread out before her. "I have four quarters—that makes a dollar." She put the quarters together in a stack.

"Plus, I have three dimes . . . ten, twenty, thirty . . . and three nickels . . . thirty-five, forty, forty-five . . . and five pennies . . . forty-six, forty-seven, forty-eight, forty-nine, fifty. So all those cents together make one dollar and fifty cents!"

"That's right! But you still need two dollars and fifty cents more before you have four dollars," Robin reminded her sister.

Jennie's face fell. "How can I get that much money?"

"Why don't you ask Dad if you can do some extra chores to earn money?" suggested Robin.

"That's a great idea!" said Jennie.

Jennie went to her father. "Dad, do you have any chores I can do to earn two dollars and fifty cents?"

"Sure," said Jennie's dad. "I've got lots of things to do around the yard. You can help me rake the leaves."

When they were done, Jennie's dad gave her a big hug and three one-dollar bills. "Here's the money you need, plus a little extra for being such a good worker!"

"Thanks, Dad," Jennie said happily. "Now I have four dollars and fifty cents. That's enough for my fish! Can we please go back to the pet store?"

In the pet store, Jennie walked up to the counter. "I'd like to buy the fish now, please," she said. She counted out the four dollars and gave it to the shopkeeper.

"Why, you learned how to count money!" said the shopkeeper, smiling.

"Yes, I did," Jennie replied proudly. "And I earned the money myself. I even saved some money for next time. I'll be back sometime soon—you can *count* on it!"